How do you express something that is important to you?

FROM ME TO YOU

by Adrienne M. Frater
illustrated by Antonio Vincenti

Chapter 1
POOR JOSH

I was riding my bike home when an ambulance passed me. The siren on the ambulance was wailing.

"Josh had an accident. He fell off his skateboard and broke his leg," Mom said when I got home.

I responded, "That's terrible! I saw the ambulance on my way home." Josh lives next door. He's like a brother to me.

At supper that night, I stared at my plate. "Not hungry?" Dad signed to me. He looked concerned.

My dad is deaf, but he can read lips and use sign language. "I just can't stop thinking about Josh," I responded.

"I'm sure he'll be okay, Gina," Dad replied.

siren

Gina

AMBULANCE
dial | 911

The next day, I found out that Josh had broken his femur, the bone above his knee. Josh is in traction. I asked Josh's mom what traction meant.

She explained what happens. "First, the doctor gives Josh an anesthetic so he doesn't feel any pain. Then, the doctor puts a pin through his femur. Cables attached to the pin hold his leg up in a sling."

I must have looked pale because Josh's mom reassured me. "Josh is fine, Gina. He just has to stay in the hospital for a few weeks." It sounded terrible. Josh is a sporty guy. He must feel trapped lying in bed all day.

I wanted to visit Josh, but the hospital is far away. Mom is busy with my new baby sister, and Dad is busy with his gardening business. I doubted they could take me. Luckily, Josh's mom asked me to go with them to see Josh on the weekend.

That evening I thought about visiting Josh at the hospital. I wanted to get a present, but that would be difficult for me.

I didn't want to ask Dad for money because his business is slow at this time of the year. Then I saw the answer to my problem.

I had spotted a mobile hanging in the window. I had made that mobile in kindergarten. As I watched the mobile gently spin, I got an idea for a present.

My parents always like the presents I make for them. They told me that handmade presents are more meaningful than something you buy from a store because they are an expression of your feelings. I decided to make a mobile for Josh that contains the memories of our friendship.

Josh and I have known each other all of our lives. I wanted Josh to remember the fun times. Now I had to choose which memories to include in the mobile.

"I'll ask his family and his other friends for ideas," I decided.

STOP AND CHECK

Why does Gina decide to make Josh a mobile?

Chapter 2
MY IDEA

It was Tuesday. I had four days until the visit to see Josh, so I started working on the mobile in the morning.

I asked Josh's friend Hunter what they liked to do together. Hunter blushed and mumbled. "What did you say?" I asked.

"We play superheroes," Hunter said a little louder.

"Cool," I said and smiled. Josh and I like to play superheroes sometimes, too.

That night I looked for things I needed to make the mobile. Finally, I found one thing under my bed.

The next day, I asked Josh's older sister, "Sarah, what do you and Josh like to do together?"

"Nothing much now, but he used to enjoy dangling bugs and spiders in front of me. It scared me. Is that any help?"

"It sure is," I laughed.

5

I can't take a live bug to the hospital, but there is something else I can take. I went out to the garden and found what I needed.

That afternoon I asked Josh's mom, "What do you and Josh like to do together?"

She answered, "These days Josh really likes to cook with me. He likes cooking as much as you do."

My Italian grandmother taught me how to make pasta and pizza. One day I had taught Josh to make pasta. I decided that when Josh gets home, I'll teach him how to make pizza, too. That night, I looked in the pantry to find more materials for the mobile.

dish towel

pasta

ocean

shell

sand

On Thursday I looked at the paintings I had made. Josh had encouraged me to use my imagination, and now my paintings have lots of color.

I thought to myself, "Sometimes I teach Josh, and other times Josh teaches me."

Later that evening, I remembered something else that Josh and I like to do together. I signed to Dad, "Do you want to take a walk on the beach?"

"Sure," he signed back. "<u>It's</u> low tide now."

My dad and I raced each other to the beach. I ran around like a dog searching for its bone. Some people think our beach is barren, but if you look closely enough, there are tons of living things in the sand.

Language Detective	<u>It's</u> is a contraction of "it is." Find the homophone for <u>it's</u> on this page.

I looked through sticks and shells and seaweed, but I didn't see anything I wanted. Then I saw the perfect thing for the mobile, and it made me laugh!

Josh and I always played a searching game at the beach. The winner was the one who found the weirdest thing. If Josh were here today, I would definitely win the game with what I had found.

By Friday the mobile was almost done. I threaded each object and tied it with a knot. Next, I balanced the objects on the frame. Finally, I hung the mobile and watched it twirl.

Something wasn't right. I stared at the mobile to determine what was missing. Something that was important to Josh was not on the mobile.

STOP AND CHECK

How does Gina decide what to put on the mobile?

Chapter 3
SHOULD I OR SHOULD I NOT?

"I'm going to talk to Josh's dad," I told Mom. I knew that Josh loved to skateboard with his friends. He skated with his dad, too, in their yard. His dad even built the skate ramp in their backyard. Josh had broken his leg when he fell off the skate ramp.

At Josh's house, his dad greeted me. Then he asked, "What is it, Gina?"

I told him about the mobile. Then I said, "It doesn't seem right to make a memory mobile without his favorite activity. But since the accident, I don't know whether I should include something to represent skateboarding."

Josh's dad replied, "Josh loves skateboarding. He will definitely be back on his skateboard as quickly as he can. You should include skateboarding." He paused, then said, "Come with me."

Josh's dad took me to his toolshed. It was a wonderful, dusty old place. The shed contained lots of different things. Josh and I had spent hours in this shed, <u>poking around</u> among the plumes of dust. It was like opening a Christmas stocking.

"Look in there." Josh's dad pointed to a box of old skateboard parts. I looked through the box, but everything was too heavy to hang on a mobile.

Then I held up something large. "Can I use this?"

"It's yours," Josh's dad answered.

"Thank you!" I said.

> **In Other Words** exploring. En español, *poking around* quiere decir *husmeando.*

skateboard wheel

box

The next morning, I found my dad before he left for work. "Please come," I signed to him. We went to his toolshed, and I explained what I wanted. Dad found it right away.

I carefully wrapped the presents and then got ready to go to the hospital. "Give these to Josh for me," Mom said. She handed me a container full of cookies she had baked.

"Lucky Josh!" I said and carried the cookies and gifts to Josh's house.

We arrived at the hospital about an hour later. There were small yellow ducks painted on the hospital floor. They were signs to the children's ward. We followed the signs.

The children's ward was completely different from what I had imagined. Most of the children were running around or walking with crutches. Everyone was making a lot of noise. Josh was the only patient with a grumpy look on his face.

"Hi, Josh," his parents and I said at the same time.

STOP AND CHECK

Why does Gina want to talk to Josh's dad?

Chapter 4
WHAT WILL JOSH THINK?

As I approached his bed, I tried not to look at Josh's broken leg, but I could see the traction cables attached to a frame over the bed. They looked scary.

I smiled and said, "Hi, Josh. How is <u>your</u> leg?"

Josh said, "I'm okay. You don't look okay, though. You're as white as a sheet!"

"Sorry. I don't like hospitals or broken bones very much," I said.

"Then I should show you my leg so you can stop worrying." I had to look where Josh was pointing.

"This is the pin." Josh pulled back the sheet and showed me. "And these cables go from the pin to the weight." Josh pointed to the end of the bed. "If you look down there, you can see the weight that keeps my femur straight. The weight takes the pressure off the bone so it can heal."

Language Detective	<u>Your</u> is a possessive pronoun. Find a homophone for <u>your</u> on this page.

Josh seemed to be feeling better because he reached for his presents. He opened the container of cookies. "Chocolate chip! Fantastic! And what's this?"

mobile

traction frame

I <u>crossed</u> <u>my fingers</u> while Josh unwrapped the mobile. "It's something I made. It's a memory mobile. See?" I hung the mobile on the traction frame.

Josh stared at the mobile for so long that I started to wonder if he hated it. I watched him look at the little superhero model, the piece of pasta, the paintbrush, the snail shell, and the false teeth with sand from the beach. They slowly spun around.

Then Josh began to laugh, and I knew he understood. But when he stopped laughing, he started to frown again.

In Other Words hoped that he would like the gift. En español, *crossed my fingers* quiere decir *espero que pase.*

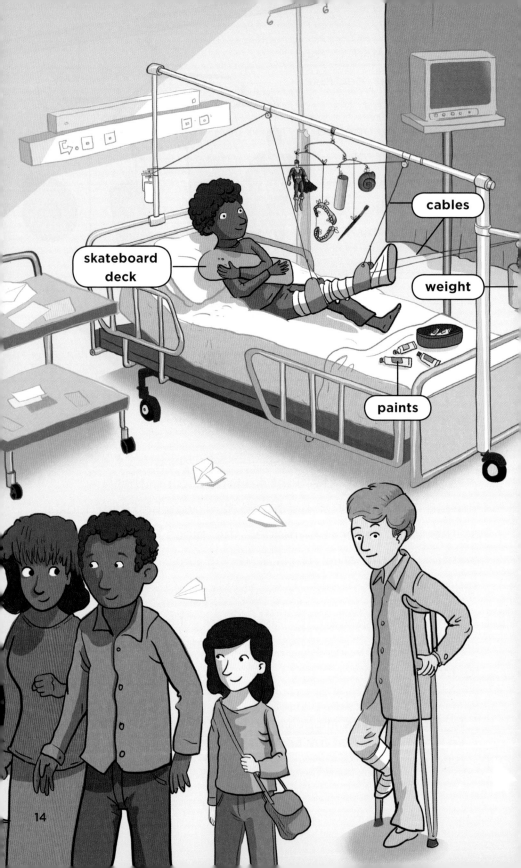

skateboard deck

cables

weight

paints

14

I suspected Josh was thinking about having to stay in the hospital, but I only said, "Time for the second present!" I passed the other package to Josh.

From the shape of the package, Josh could tell right away what was inside.

"Open it," I urged. Josh unwrapped the old skateboard deck.

"There's more," I said and passed him a plastic bag. Inside the bag was a box of paints and a paintbrush.

"Am I supposed to decorate the deck?" Josh asked.

"It's called skateboard art," I told him.

Josh replied, "Oh, cool!"

"After your leg heals, you'll have the brightest board on the street," Josh's dad said.

When it was time to go home, the cookies were all gone and Josh was holding the skateboard deck. I hoped that my presents let Josh know that he had lots of good things to look forward to when he recovered.

STOP AND CHECK

Describe Josh at the hospital.

Summarize

Use important details to summarize *From Me to You.* Your graphic organizer may help you.

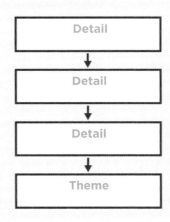

Detail

↓

Detail

↓

Detail

↓

Theme

Text Evidence

1. How do you know that this story is realistic fiction?
GENRE

2. How did Gina choose the items for the mobile? How do her choices convey the theme of the story?
THEME

3. What simile does the author use to describe how Gina runs on page 7? Explain the comparison.
SIMILE AND METAPHOR

4. Reread the last paragraph on page 15. Write about what Gina thinks. How do her thoughts communicate the theme of the story? WRITE ABOUT READING

Compare Texts

Read a poem that expresses how Josh feels in the hospital.

Sssh!

It's quiet in the ward.

The patients are sleeping,

all except me.

Sssh! says the nurse.

It's time you were asleep.

Eyes wide open,

I stare at the dark.

I stare at the dark and think

about the world outside,

waiting for my leg to mend.

I think about skateboarding

and the places I'll go—

the beach, the skate park, the mall.

Sssh! says the nurse.

It's time you were asleep.

I think about the places I'll go

and who will go with me.

I think about Gina, my family, my friends.

My eyelids droop ... drop down.

I see sunshine, sailboats, and sand.

Ah! says the nurse.

He's asleep.

Make Connections

How does the poem express what is important to Josh? ESSENTIAL QUESTION

Compare the way Gina expresses her feelings in *From Me to You* with the way Josh expresses his feelings in *Sssh!* TEXT TO TEXT

Focus on Literary Elements

Alliteration Alliteration is the repetition of the same beginning consonant sound in two or more words near each other. Poets often use alliteration to make the words or lines in a poem flow in a musical way.

Read and Find In *Sssh!*, the author uses alliteration several times. In the eighth verse, for example, the *d* sound is repeated in "droop....drop down," connecting the three words. Look for more instances of alliteration in the poem.

Your Turn

With a partner, write a poem using alliteration. List three or four things you would put on a memory mobile for your classmates. Brainstorm words and phrases that describe the item. The descriptive words you choose should begin with the same sound as the item. For example, "battered baseball." Read the poem aloud to the class.